Batting
Coach

LES ED

CPA – Motiva

An Educator Fo

Self
Esteem

THE B◎

70 Stone Ho.
Tunnelton, WV 26444

(304) 892-2830

email: lvedinger@yahoo.com
www.bopshop.tk

Umpire
Maker

Successful
Failures

Strike Three,
But
Still Swinging

6-24-12

Mary,

I hope you
enjoy this little
Book.
God Bless.

Les Colvqin

Strike Three,
But
Still Swinging

LES and SHARON EDINGER

Library of Congress Control Number: 2009901536
ISBN: Hardcover   978-1-4415-1301-4
                   Softcover   978-1-4415-1300-7

This book was printed in the United States of America.

To order additional copies of this book, contact:
Xlibris Corporation
1-888-795-4274
www.Xlibris.com
Orders@Xlibris.com
56486

CONTENTS

† In baseball there is an umpire to rule on every play
He calls you out or safe at home as you come to bat each day.
In life, you're the umpire and some may curse and shout
But you're the one that calls the shots, only you can call you out.

In baseball you get three strikes, and the umpire will not flinch
For when the man in blue has spoken, you're headed for the bench.
In life your strikes aren't counted as you seek to gain your fame
As long as you keep swinging, you're a credit to the game.
Strike Three but Still Swinging

INTRODUCTION

BASEBALL IS A wonderful game. I spent countless hours on the vacant lot with the pals of my childhood. My mother could find me there throughout most of the summer as well as every evening after school. As I got older, I participated in the Little League and Babe Ruth summer programs in Elkins, West (by gosh!) Virginia. That *by gosh* was inserted to emphasize that Elkins is not a town in the Commonwealth of Virginia. Elkins is in West Virginia.

Later in high school I continued to play the game. I never developed into a super athlete, but I had some good memories, and the time spent on the diamond kept me out of trouble. Participating in those years of baseball taught me a great deal about sportsmanship, teamwork, friendship, and cooperation. I also learned a little about umpires. They are not perfect; some of them need glasses, and you might as well get water to flow uphill as to get one of them to change a decision about a call. However, in all fairness to the umps of the world, they are an essential part of the game of baseball. They keep the game moving, provide law and order during the contest, and provide someone other than players to be the target of boos and jeers. God bless the umps.

The rules of baseball state that a batter is allowed three strikes and, upon receiving the third one, is ruled *out* and must return to the bench. The ump helps determine what is considered a strike and, upon the third one, notifies the batter that he or she is out. That is baseball, and that will be baseball as long as it is called America's Favorite Pastime.

But baseball is only a game. It only lasts nine innings, and this book is about life, and our life lasts an entire lifetime. In baseball a batter only gets three strikes and is called out; in life things are a great deal different. First of all, in life, there is no person wearing a blue suit, a chest protector, and a mask following us around. In life, we are our own umpires, and we have no limit to the strikes we are allotted. It doesn't matter if we miss the ball or fail a thousand times; as long as we don't call ourselves out by quitting, we can continue to try and try and try again until we are successful with whatever we are trying to accomplish.

Unfortunately, there are far too many people that do not believe this. Too many people quit their projects, give up on their dreams, and never reach their full potential because they consider certain key people in their lives as umpires. Some children are raised by parents who have told them repeatedly that they can't do certain things. Some people allow brothers and sisters to discourage them. For others, it is a neighbor or a business associate that is hurling those negative comments. Even our closest friends unknowingly have killed our dreams or have prevented us from progressing because we place so much emphasis on their opinions.

CHAPTER I

Believe in Yourself

THE FIRST STEP in becoming our own umpires is to believe in ourselves. Believe in yourself. You are a talented, gifted, and unique individual. You are a human being. All human beings are different in that they each have unique talents, gifts, dreams, and interests; but all humans have one thing in common. They have the ability to think, and with this ability, they can achieve equally great and remarkable things in their lives as any of the great ones in history. If you have a desire and dream to accomplish something, you can succeed. It probably won't happen instantaneously, but it will happen if you keep trying.

As I have already mentioned, however, too many people do not believe this because of the many put-downs they have received from others. Too many people are being conditioned by others as elephants are being conditioned by circus people. Have you ever wondered what keeps an eight-thousand-pound giant anchored to a stake by only a small chain or piece of rope?

Elephants and You

The elephant, so strong, so majestic, so grand
The world says he doesn't forget;
But he isn't as bright as we once thought he was;
I am telling you this with regret.

For as a small baby calf about three hundred pounds
He is staked by a very strong rope;
He can pull tug and strain without any gain
Till he gives up all chances of hope.

Then day after day, month after month
Trying to break loose, run, and be free;
He finally accepts that he isn't so hept
And proclaims, "Oh, Fiddle-de dee."

And then as he grows to ten thousand pounds
A string replaces the rope;
But the mammoth's huge brain thinks the string is a chain
And he still can't break free, the poor dope.

And so many kids are treated this way
By parents and neighbors and peers;
Many others at times have acted unkind
And have put kids down through the years.

They are told they're not smart
That they don't have the heart;
It's no use to be mighty and bold
That they are lazy and slow.
And as these kids grow
They begin to believe what they're told.

But there are others who think you are special, my friend
There are others who will help you along;
There are others who'll say, "Believe in Yourself
Do good and never do wrong."

If you can believe all the good you possess
And never forget for a minute;
Then you can achieve what the world has in store
LOOK UP, THE SKY IS THE LIMIT!

LES AND SHARON EDINGER

Millions of people make two great mistakes according to Dr. David Schwartz. In his classic book, *The Magic of Thinking Big*, Dr. Schwartz says that people tend to overestimate the other person's intelligence, and they also underestimate their own. It is a common mistake by most people to suppose that the rich man living in our neighborhood is much smarter than us. Another common error is that he is endowed with super thinking abilities that we could never develop. Nothing could be farther from the truth. Don't sell yourself short. The rich, the famous, the leaders in our society are really no smarter or better than anyone else. They do posses two or three habits that most people have not developed. One of these is the habit of believing in themselves.

Suppose that you just bought a brand-new Cadillac fully loaded with accessories. Perhaps you paid in excess of $30,000. Let us also suppose that one of your friends asked you for a ride downtown and you said yes. How would you feel if your good buddy entered your car with shoes covered with mud? How would you feel if he also proceeded to dump a full bag of shelled peanuts into your backseat? I would bet that you would have a few unkind words for your friend, and you might even ask him to get out and call a cab. Not many people would put up with such rudeness, not even from a friend. If he is that inconsiderate; he deserves to walk.

Now, what if a friend, neighbor, or guest entered your house and proceeded to act in a similar manner. Just close your eyes and picture one of your acquaintances enter your house and immediately commence to spit upon your floor or pick up a crayon and begin to write on your walls. If he walked over to your living room sofa and began to scrape off the mud from his shoes, would you say anything to him? If you wouldn't, what about your mother or wife or husband, depending on your situation?

I think that you would agree with me that most people would speak up and stop a ridiculous situation like the one I just described. I would also probably do some tossing. Yet how many times in your life have you allowed people to place dirt, garbage, or just plain junk into your mind. When people begin to put us down, they have gone too far. When they commence to tell us that we are too stupid or too inexperienced or just too old or too young, they have gone too far. Anytime a friend, relative, neighbor, or peer begins to place negative ideas into our minds that might distract us from something that we are trying to accomplish, they have overstepped their bounds. Do not listen to them. If you truly want to accomplish something and are willing to do what it takes to accomplish that something, then rest assured, you can do it. You can succeed.

Don't Dump on Me

The guests have arrived at your house tonight
For dinner and an evening of fun;
They stand at the door with their trash and implore
If the laughter and games have begun.

And as they enter your door, they gaze at the floor
With the carpet so azure and new;
Then dump on its threads some moldy old bread
And the last of last evening's beef stew.

Then as they mingle with guests, they deposit the rest
Of the garbage that filled up their packs;
Dumping food here and there, a melon, a pear
And greasy potato chip sacks.

Would you welcome such guests for an evening of rest
Embrace them and be ever so kind?
Or would you move their two feet outside in the street,
Say good night and kick their behinds.

I wouldn't enjoy a girl or boy
Who entered my house spreading such trash;
I would show them who's who, and I believe you would too
Throw them out, and I mean in a flash.

Yet how often our friends and even our kin
Dump garbage and trash in our minds;
When they tell us we're crazy, got no chance or just lazy
These friends are really unkind.

LES AND SHARON EDINGER

Don't let anyone start and say you're not smart,
That you're slow, you're a fool, you can't win;
Just believe that you can, saying special I am
And you'll see, you'll win in the end.

We probably cannot be experts in every area of life since we all have different interests and desires. Albert Einstein was a whiz in science and math, but he may have had a difficult time putting a water pump on his car. Thomas Edison was unsurpassed in creating new devices that made life easier and more enjoyable, but I doubt if he would have been a terrific opera singer. That was not his so-called cup of tea. One of the main reasons that Edison and Einstein excelled was that they chose areas in life where they had high interest. Those areas are where these two famous people focused all their time and talents.

When we choose an area that we are highly interested in and have a solid belief that we can succeed in that area, then nothing in the world can stop us from achieving success except ourselves. If others have succeeded in certain fields, then so can we, and *we* includes you. Albert Einstein, Thomas Edison, Billy Graham, Mary Tyler Moore, Michael Jordan, Larry King, and Harry Truman were all human beings; and so are you.

The Human Race

Be good to yourself, you really deserve it
There is no one exactly like you;
For you are unique, gifted, and special
I hope you agree with me too.

Don't put yourself down, speak bad of your life
But be pleased when you look at your face;
For you, Trevino, Lou Gehrig, and Lincoln
All belong to the same human race.

How valuable are you? How much are you worth? How priceless is a human being? I truly believe that you are priceless. The creator is always worth more than that which he or she creates. Since it was man that created all the gadgets and inventions in this world, I feel that men and women are more valuable than them all.

Men and women have dominion over all the animals. Men train horses to race, and some of these horses sell for over a million dollars. Some retired racehorses that are used for stud bring their owner over $8,000,000 a year. There are some prize coonhounds that have been trained to be champion hunters and are worth thousands of dollars. Besides racing and hunting, some animals have been taught to ride bicycles, find buried people, perform at Sea World, protect the innocent, apprehend criminals, sniff out drugs and numerous other things. Some of them would bring thousands of dollars on the market. Yet none of these things would be possible if it were not for a human.

It is a human that trains and rides the horse. It is a human that trains that police dog to distinguish the difference between soap and cocaine. It is a human that trains the whales. None of these animals train their human owners and then make money for their personal needs. There are thousands of species of animals on this planet, and the human being alone has the ability to think. We do not see whales walking on any downtown street. We do not see the mighty eagle swimming 150 feet below the surface. Except for Rudolph and eight of his buddies, we do not see deer or bears flying two miles above the surface of this earth. No, only a human has the ability to move out of his natural environment and survive. Why, because he has the ability to think, reason, and be creative. This makes man the most valuable creature on the face of the planet. Never forget how priceless you are. You can be anything you truly desire. You can go anywhere you truly desire, and you can create anything you truly desire. Just believe in yourself.

The Race Horse

The man wrote a check for one million dollars
His savings for forty-five years;
And purchased Ms. Champion, a real thoroughbred breed
A horse we all would revere.

LES AND SHARON EDINGER

Then he dreamed of Kentucky and the Derby in May
Of the Belmont and Preakness, of course;
A Triple Crown winner would pay for his dinner
With plenty of checks to endorse.

He took his horse home, bound to treat it like family
Ms. Champion was just one of the clan;
But he fed her and fed her all she could eat
Till her waistline began to expand.

Then he let her drink coffee and smoke cigarettes
Till three in the morning each night;
And they traveled through town, searching around
For a stallion that Champion could fight.

Then finally in May on the great Derby Day
He knew that she couldn't be beat;
But as the jockey was counting on her back to start mounting,
She whinnied, falling dead at his feet.

You know, it really was sad to treat a thoroughbred bad
That horse could have been a real champ;
But the owner so cruel was really a fool
And today, she's just glue on a stamp.

But listen, dear friend, to this thought at the end
Of this poem of misery and woe;
That horsey not spared was nothing compared
To you, for you are a pro.

You are worth so much more than any old horse
Ten million, a billion, or more;
Take care of yourself, you jolly young elf,
For the riches of life are in store.

Get plenty of rest and study your best
Eat wisely and exercise too;
Put a smile on your face and finish life's race,
The world is counting on you.

Yes, the world is counting on you, but even more important than that statement is this one. You are counting on you. If you don't look after yourself, no one else will. You need to count on yourself and make sure that you are doing the best things that will help you now and in your future. You definitely have the skills and abilities to enrich your life and the lives of others. Everyone has that ability. It is a God-given gift. I learned that lesson years ago as a sophomore in high school from a substitute teacher.

As I remember, the teacher told us of an experience from his life fifty years earlier. He was a senior in high school, and his class was sponsoring a talent show. Fliers went up all over the school, and the students were signing up for the big night of entertainment. Some were going to dance. Some were going to sing or play musical instruments. Others would twirl batons, recite poetry, perform magic tricks, juggle, and exhibit a variety of other talents.

Our teacher told us that a week before the show, Joey signed up to entertain those in attendance. This caused a great deal of concern for our teacher and his classmates. He explained that Joey was a very nice, well-liked individual, but he was somewhat slow in learning. Today, they would say that he was educationally impaired; back then the word was *retarded*. Everyone felt sorry for Joey, for they knew that he would be introduced, would walk out on the stage, stand for a few minutes, and do nothing. What could he do? This would only support what all the classmates already knew; he was somewhat disabled. Poor Joey. But no one had the heart to talk him out of trying because Joey was excited about the evening.

The evening of the performance finally arrived, and the talent show was a big success. The audience enjoyed the singers, dancers, magicians, and all the other talented performers. Then Joey was introduced, and he walked to center stage. He stood there for about thirty seconds and slowly announced that he would like to roll for them. With that introduction, Joey sat on the stage, lowered his head, put his arms under his legs, and formed a small human ball. Joey then proceeded to roll around the stage. In about thirty more seconds, the entire audience rose to their feet and

LES AND SHARON EDINGER

gave him the loudest ovation of the evening. With the cheers, the clapping, and the whistles, Joey continued to roll around and around and around that stage.

Our teacher told us that day, and I believed him and always will, that all humans can do something unique and special; and we need to discover just what it is in our own lives. Joey may have had some handicaps; but that night, on a high school stage in West Virginia, he convinced those in attendance that he was one of the world's greatest rollers. Joey had the ability to entertain those people that night, and even though I have never met him, his story inspires me to this very day.

That story made quite an impression on my mind when it was told to me by that substitute teacher, Mr. Frank "Coach" Wimer. Coach Wimer was at that time a retired teacher and only substituted as needed by the school board. He was a member of the West Virginia Sports Hall of Fame and was known nationally by many sports figures. Again, that story was special to me the minute I heard it, but it was forever engraved into my memory some fifteen years later when Coach Wimer and his lovely wife were brutally murdered. Coach Wimer may be gone from this world, but his teachings continue to influence my life and the lives of many others.

Joey in the above story had some handicaps. He definitely was lacking in many skills and talents that the other classmates had. But Joey did not worry about things that he did not have; he just concentrated on the talents that he did have and was able to entertain that night. Do you concentrate on your own talents and skills, or do you spend your time wishing that you had the skills and talents of others?

You already possess enough talents and abilities to do far more than you realize. You are already contributing a great deal to our society, and once you truly get into the habit of believing in yourself, you will be doing a great deal more. So don't worry about the talents and skills of others; concentrate on your own. Have you ever wondered what life would be like if God allowed only the best birds to sing? I have a feeling that our forests and neighborhoods would be a lot quieter. We need all of our feathered friends to make the beautiful music we hear from spring to winter—all of them, with no exceptions. It is the same with human beings; we all contribute, and each of us can do our part for the good of all the others.

Let Everyone Sing

Let John give the speech for he's older and wiser
And they say he's a good-looking guy;
Let Jane sing the solo during choir today
For I know that she just isn't shy.

I won't bother to add my point of view
For I might put my foot in my mouth;
And I'll appear just as funny as Brer Rabbit the Bunny
In the stories that were told in the South.

Now hold it right there for you don't understand
That they are no different from you;
Don't sell yourself short for the others aren't perfect
They are comparing and worrying too.

When you can, take a walk in the country someday
And listen real early in morn;
To the birds on the hill with their music so shrill
As the sun greets the day that is born.

You can hear the blue jays, the sparrows, and wrens
With the robins as they are making their nests;
And the finches so small in the trees standing tall
All doing what birdies do best.

Some whistle a tune, some peck at the trees
Others crow, some chatter or call;
And joining together surrounding the heather
It sounds like they're having a ball.

LES AND SHARON EDINGER

Now suppose God allowed just the best birds to sing
And the others had nothing to say;
How lonely and dreary the forest would be
It really would be a sad day.

But the way that it is, all the birds have a chance
To quack, chirp, whistle, or sing;
And because they are different, they all harmonize
With a heavenly musical ring.

So don't worry if John speaks better than you
Just give it your best doggone try;
Adding your flair as the birds of the air,
Will bring more blue to your sky.

Reach around behind you, grab yourself by the seat of your britches, and pull yourself off the bench of life. Get out there and participate in life and give it your best shot. Don't rely on other people, thinking that they are better, for they are not. You have what it takes to give something special to your family, community, and nation. Too many people wait on others to speak up or wait for them to carry the baton when we could do it just as well or better. As these four following lines suggest, do it yourself:

But, friends, you are sadly mistaken
For the boys know down on the farm;
That the best place to find a strong helping hand
Is to look at the end of your arm.

What do successful people look like? Where do successful people live? What race produces successful people? Close your eyes and picture a successful person. Is that person a male or female? What is the nationality of a successful person? So much for the questions. The truth is that successful people live everywhere on earth. All races produce successful people as well as all nations. There are successful women as well as successful men.

My point here is that successful people are found all over the world from a variety of nations and from a variety of races. Whatever age you are at the present, an enormous number of people who have excelled in some area are living today at that very same age. The same goes for your sex, race, height, origin, or social status. None of these things are that critical in determining if you have what it takes to excel. What does matter is if you truly have faith in yourself.

Balloons

He was selling balloons at the beach one day
As the waves rolled onto the shore;
There were several children waiting their turn
At his portable seaside store.

There were red and yellow and green balloons
And blue ones along with some white;
And black ones too with the darkest of hue
As if seen on a moonless night.

As fast as he could he accepted the quarters
Then handed the balloons to the kids;
For forty-five minutes he emptied his wagon
Till the last from his rack he undid.

And this last balloon which was black and pretty
He gave to a handsome young boy;
Then closing his shop he headed for home
With thoughts of an evening of joy.

"Oh, mister, please wait, for I have a question."
And the man turned his head and looked down;
At the last little boy who had bought a balloon,
He was wearing his face in a frown.

LES AND SHARON EDINGER

"What do you want?" the kindly man asked
As the boy looked up from below.
"Dear sir, before you leave for the evening
There is something that I just have to know."

"If I would release my new black balloon
And allow it to climb in the sky;
Would it go just as far as the other balloons
Would my black one go just as high?"

The man bent down and patted his shoulder
Then explained to this child full of thought;
"The balloons will soar high, way up in the sky
Including the black one you bought.

"It matters not of the color, my friend,
If you want to soar in the skies;
But it is what is inside of balloon or of man
That causes them both to rise."

No, it doesn't matter what your color, sex, height, looks, nationality, family background, age, financial status, or your past history is, my friend. What does matter is that deep inside of yourself, deep within your mind and heart, you truly believe in your own abilities. With that belief and with God's support, you can accomplish anything in life that you truly desire.

Albert Einstein was a remarkable person who had an extremely inquisitive mind. He was always searching for more answers. He was truly an example of a lifelong student. He read, studied, and experimented year after year; and today people refer to him as a genius. They are right; he was.

The same can be said for George Washington Carver and Thomas Edison. They revolutionized the world with their inventions and creations. They also can be listed in the world's Hall of Fame and be considered geniuses.

As great as the three men were, however, they were still just human beings like you and me. They did not have three brains and seven sets of arms and legs. They had only what each of us has—a typical human body and mind.

Once again, they did have something all other great people possess—the basic belief that they could succeed with an invention, a discovery, or a project. They had many ideas running through their heads just as your mind has thoughts, ideas, and dreams. What do most people do with their ideas and dreams? They procrastinate, not taking any action until that idea no longer rises to the surface of their conscious thought. They tell themselves, "That idea can't be a very good one because I thought of it."

What did Einstein, Carver, and Edison do? When they had an idea, they followed through with it. They tested it out, asked questions, read books, implemented a plan, and brought into reality what at one time was only a thought. That is why they are referred to as geniuses. That is exactly why they were geniuses. They not only had ideas but also did something about them.

Today in America, we are battling with our natural resources. We have wasted water, forests, minerals, and even the air we breathe. But the greatest of all resources that we have wasted is our minds. What are you wasting?

What a Waste

Americans are facing so many problems
Oh where, oh where to begin;
The air that we breathe, the filth in our streams
And our forests may come to an end.

What a shame to waste the things that God gave us
When they are gone, they are hard to restore;
And many unique and beautiful creations
Exist only in a word we call *yore*.

But, friend, there is one thing much worse than the others
The greatest of wastes of mankind;
It is sad but it's true and I'm telling you
Too many are wasting their minds.

Many women and men pass away from this earth
Never using the skills of their brain;
To find a cure that is sure to end a disease
And relieve a person from pain.

LES AND SHARON EDINGER

So don't waste the power to create and discover
Bach, Einstein, Whitman, and You
Are of the same race, this fact just embrace
And the road to greatness pursue!!!

Too many people go to their graves in this country with their music still in their heads; with their cures for diseases still in their heads; and with inventions, plays, bridges, jokes, buildings, spacecraft, and thousands of other things still in their heads. What a waste! Please, don't waste your thoughts and ideas. The world needs just what you have to contribute.

Al, George, and Tom

Little Al and his friend were two of a kind
In a number of ways you might say;
They both liked to eat and they both liked to read
And they both remained active all day.

They read the same books and liked the same movies
And played the same games in the street;
As scholars at school, neither one was a fool
But Al is the one called unique.

He became famous as a teacher of science
And in math, he proved he was sage;
With his theory of energy and mass and the rest
Came the birth of the nuclear age.

And Tom had some friends that were friendly and bright
And like Tom they had dreams of their own;
But Tom is the one that we think of each night
When we turn the lights on in our home.

And George had some pals that we couldn't call dummies
Though they danced to their own sort of tune;
But they ate the peanuts while dear Dr. Carver
Worked wonders with this tiny legume.

These men are called genius for the work they completed
Their ideas help mankind every day;
But they are not famous for their ideas alone,
No, they acted in their own special way.

Many people and perhaps you are one
Have ideas that really aren't bad;
But lacking faith in themselves and their work
They drop them, now isn't that sad.

A man we call genius and many of us
Are no different in except in one fact;
When we have a thought, we say, "Who am I?"
But a genius has the courage to act.

A brilliant idea that dies in one's mind
Is worthless to all sisters and brothers;
But a simple idea that gets acted upon
Can enrich perhaps millions of others.

Many people have similar experiences as the ugly duckling. That bird thought he was ugly, inferior, and worthless. Do you ever feel that way? Many of the great ones in history had those feelings. Harry Truman had to wear glasses as a small boy and didn't participate in the rough-and-tumble games as his pals in school. Since Eleanor Roosevelt was not a very beautiful woman, she tended to be shy and passive, allowing other people to stand in the spotlight.

As time passed, however, these people began to transform into very productive citizens and were loved and admired by millions. Harry Truman became a World War I veteran, a U.S. senator, and later the president of the United States of America. Eleanor Roosevelt's looks never changed, but her caring personality and warm disposition won the hearts of Americans from coast to coast. To many people, you could not find another American more beautiful than Mrs. Roosevelt

Many times we get down on ourselves and begin to think like that ugly duckling. We are too slow, too short, too stupid, or something else. If only we could have the looks, the talents, the backgrounds, or the money of someone else. If we only had those things, then we could do something special. But,

LES AND SHARON EDINGER

friends, the truth is you are already something special. Perhaps your time has not yet come. Those famous people didn't become famous overnight. Perhaps you still have lessons to learn, skills to develop, and opportunities that have not yet knocked on your door. Truman and Roosevelt eventually developed a basic belief in their own talents and capabilities. When you truly feel that way about yourself, you will have won over half the battle.

The Swan

You remember I'm sure the duck that was ugly
That later turned into a swan;
Changed from homely to a most beautiful bird
As if touched by a magical wand.

Have you ever felt like the duckling so small
That others were better than you?
That others can gain wealth, beauty, and fame
But you can't. Well, that just isn't true.

Whoever you are or wherever you live
You can have all that life has in store;
But you have to prepare and study with care
Then opportunity will open its door.

Do you come from the city midst violence and crime?
Or from a farm raising cattle and wheat?
Are you the child of a sailor that lives near the coast?
Or are you raised in a desert of heat?

Are you raised in a home with only one parent?
Are you needing more money to spend?
Are you tired of living in a building complex?
Do you long for a garden to tend?

Then starting today say farewell to the past
And begin by living this rule;
To study and learn, do yourself a good turn
By staying and excelling in school.

Be a teacher, a preacher, an FBI man
Be a pilot that soars in the sky;
Be a doctor or dentist or inquisitive chemist
Just follow that gleam in your eye.

Find someone you trust to help you along
Inferior feelings suppress;
And slowly you'll see a more versatile *me*
And you'll be a swan of success.

The army says for you to "be all that you can be," and you can be just about anything in the world that you desire deep inside. Of all the creatures on earth, the man is supreme. All animals have eyes, ears, hearts, brains, and stomachs. The man is the only creature, though, that has the ability to think, question, dream, and the ability to follow those dreams. As I bring this section of this book to an end, remember that you are something special. Just develop the habit of trusting yourself and begin saying, "If it's going to be, it's up to me." Christ said that "all things are possible to him who believeth." Believe in yourself and focus on the talents and abilities that you have, not on the things that you do not.

The Thinking Man

The man lifted a branch and the elephant a tree
The crowd gazed at the strength of the two;
Then the man moved a rock and the creature a boulder
The man was much weaker, that's true.

LES AND SHARON EDINGER

The world's fastest man and cheetah had a race
And it took five short seconds to know;
That the cheetah was moving at incredible speed
And the man far behind appeared slow.

The man climbed a cliff and challenged the eagle
To soar toward the sun all aglow;
The bird was so graceful as the man flapped his arms
Then fell to the rocks far below.

But today, my dear friends, I'll gladly point out
That a man can lift more with less strain;
Than elephant, ape, wild bears, or the ox
For the man utilizes his brain.

And a man can move faster than any old critter
He can cover more ground with his power;
Yes, a cheetah can sprint very fast on his feet
But not six hundred miles each hour.

An eagle soars high, way up in the sky
With a proud and majestic-like face;
But using his mind with the power to think
A man travels deep into space.

These creatures are naturally stronger and faster
Or can fly in the mighty jet stream;
But using his mind with his power to question;
Of earth's creatures, the man is supreme.

You don't need to rely on plain instinct, by George,
As the animals do every day;
For you have a mind that can study and reason
You are special in a special-like way.

CHAPTER II

Set Some Goals

THIS SECTION DEALS with the importance of setting goals in your life. What are some things that you would like to have? What would you like to become? What would you truly like to do? The answers to these questions are goals that you can set for yourself. By setting goals, developing and following a plan to reach them, you can realize your greatest dreams and ambitions. Without goals, we just drift through life from one day to the next, never accomplishing anything truly outstanding. With goals, we can reach Success City; without them, we usually end up in the city limits of a town called Nowhere.

Goals are to the individual as rudders are to a ship. They give direction and meaning to your life and something to look forward to each morning when you open your eyes. Without rudders, a ship is at the mercy of the waves, wind, and current. The ship would continue to move, but it would have little guarantee to reach the desired harbor. They say that a blind hog stumbles over an acorn once in a while. If a ship would be fortunate to reach the harbor it had set out for, it would only be by chance and would be no different than that blind hog.

In May of 1941, England was at war with Nazi Germany. The Germans had the largest and fastest battleship ever built by man. They named it the *Bismarck*. The English sent the HMS *Hood* to find and sink the *Bismark*. As the two ships squared away for battle, the *Bismark* hit the *Hood* with one shell, which landed where the *Hood* had its ammunition stored. With one mighty explosion, the HMS *Hood* disappeared from the surface of the sea, and the *Bismark* sailed on to continue its war of destruction on the British people.

Churchill, the courageous and inspiring prime minister of the English people, gave orders to launch an all-out war upon the *Bismark*. In a sense, he declared the *Bismark* as public enemy number 1 to England. All available ships and planes were sent out on the North Atlantic to find and then sink the menace to the seven seas. Every seaman was earnestly looking for the *Bismark*, but at the same time, many were asking themselves, "What happens when we find the *Bismark*? Will we end up like the sailors on the *Hood*?"

Finally, the *Bismark* was sighted; and torpedo planes, hoping to score a hit, dove down upon the giant. Fortunately for the British, one torpedo happened to hit the mighty battleship in the rudder. The *Bismark* still lhad its speed, its mighty fortress of guns, and all of its protective armor; but it no longer had control of its steering. It began to make circles in the water and, a few hours later, was at the mercy of the British navy. They surrounded the *Bismark* and proceeded to take target practice. The terror of the Third Reich was now at the bottom of the ocean, and the menace named *Bismark* had entered its last page in the history books.

In life, we need to have goals to give our lives direction. With goals, we determine where we will live and the type of house we will have. With goals, we determine the salary we will earn and the type of car we can purchase. With goals, we determine every truly important thing we will get out of life. Without goals, we are at the mercy of others. We are at the mercy of current events and at the mercy of the goals and objectives of others in our society. Do you want others to determine what your lifestyle will be like, or would you like to cast the deciding vote?

Leaves

Don't flutter around like leaves in the wind
Not knowing year after year;
Where you might live or the job you might have
Then stand and complain with a sneer.

But plan your life as you set a few goals
And determine just where you'll be;
And you decide where you're taking your life.
Only then will you truly be free.

Yes, plan your life. Otherwise, you will be like a driver that takes his hands off the steering wheel. The car might be in perfect condition and the road as straight as an arrow, but if he leaves his hand off the wheel too long, he is going to crash. If we don't take control of our own lives, then we are headed for trouble. Trouble may not show up today or tomorrow; but sooner or later, there it is, facing us right in the eyes.

Trouble may show up in the form of trouble with the boss or with a close friend. It might show up in the disguise as financial troubles, or it might appear as failing grades in high school or college. It might appear in a thousand different forms, but without any goals or plans to give us guidance, it most assuredly will show up at our door and demand attention.

I recall a story about a young man that refused to think for himself or make any plans for his future. He just drifted through life doing what others were doing. Finally, the day came when he was truly sorry for not taking charge of his own life, but just being sorry did not help his situation. "Of all the words of mice or men, the saddest are 'It might have been.'"

The River

His mother said no but as in the past
Her no was not a deterrent;
So he pushed off from shore in his little canoe
Bound to float downstream with the current.

He packed him a lunch and his new fishing pole
And some money to pay for the tab;
For when he got tired of floating downstream
He'd just hitch a ride home in a cab.

For an hour or two in his little canoe
He enjoyed the waters so deep;
Then drifting along he started to yawn
Continuing downstream fast asleep.

Well, this prodigal lad who wasn't all bad
Awoke when he started to snore;
Sat up in his boat and started to choke
For that's when he noticed the roar.

LES AND SHARON EDINGER

He was heard from the shore above the loud roar
Yelling, "Save me, dear Lord, I beg ya!"
For he knew he was wrong saying no to his mom
And remembering, this stream is Niagara.

Well, you might have a hunch that the fish ate his lunch
And you're right and you also should know;
That the reason he's dead, instead of using his head
He decided to just go with the flow.

We have to get in the habit of thinking for ourselves and then to set a few goals. With goals, we can accomplish more in one month than we could in twelve. Studies have shown this to be factual. Goals and plans are vital to our success and happiness in life. Imagine what it would be like to be on an airplane if the pilot had no real idea of just where he wanted to go. You might think that is a ridiculous statement, yet many people go their entire lives without setting some goals to help guide them.

First, decide what it is that you want out of life, and then make a plan to get what you want. Begin immediately to put that plan into action. Every night before you go to bed, review your goals and the things you did that day to reach them. If the things you did are taking you closer to your goal, *great*, just continue to follow through with your plans. If, however, the things you did, did not take you closer to your goals, then change your plans somewhat and try again tomorrow. If you do this consistently over time, you will be amazed at how many of your goals you are achieving.

Anthony Robbins says that airplanes en route to a destination are off course about 90 percent of the time. The pilot simply checks his/her instruments, determines exactly how much he/she is off, and corrects his/her direction until he/she is back on course again. The plane will then fly on course until air currents and human error cause the plane to drift off course again. The pilot continues to make corrections and adjustments until he/she lands safely at the designated airport.

The Pilot

The tower said all clear and the pilot began
To guide the big jet in the sky;
From New York to Paris, about six thousand miles
Flying thousands of feet in the sky.

As the plane sped along out over the ocean
It veered just little off route;
But if not corrected, the folks on the plane
Would end up in Russia no doubt.

But the pilot is no rookie and he watches the dials
Maneuvering the plane back on course;
The copilot too and the rest of the crew
The pilot's decisions endorse.

And every few minutes from New York to Paris
Dials check the plane's speed and the wind,
To assure that the flight in the dark of the night
Won't set the folks down in Berlin.

And as you pilot yourself through this life
Choose a goal to work on with cheer;
And make sure that the steps you are taking each day
Take you closer to your goal through the year.

If you act as the pilot with your eyes on your goals
Though you encounter some trials and strife;
You will surely arrive very strong and alive
With a happier outlook on life.

LES AND SHARON EDINGER

It was goals that took Japan from a nation that had been destroyed during World War II to a world economic power in just twenty years. It was goals that allowed the United States to catch up with Russia in the race for space and allowed us to land a man on the moon. This happened in less than ten years after President Kennedy issued the challenge. He would have been pleased to see that day, but he was cut down in his prime by an assassin's bullet.

It was goals that permitted Lee Iacocca to take Chrysler from the edge of failure to new heights of success in the auto industry. Goals took Mary Lou Retton from a little-known community in northern West Virginia and catapulted her to fame as a gold medalist in the Olympics. Goals have helped countless thousands to improve their lives, and they will do the same for you. The first step is to decide exactly what you want. Next, determine what you will have to do in order to get what you want. This is what we call planning. Things that are cheap are seldom any good, and the best in life is seldom cheap. Therefore, we need to prepare plans to get the things we want, and then we need to work those plans. *Be prepared to work.* The more difficult the struggle to reach our goals, the more rewarding will be our victory.

Work

A thought to remember to help you obtain
True riches of life like health, wealth, and fame;
Remember this fact for it's more than a hunch,
Work hard all your life, for there's no free lunch.

Review your goals every day and follow your plan. If you do this consistently, you will eventually reach your goal. If you come up with an idea of something you would like to have and do nothing more than think about it from time to time, all you are doing is wishing. Someone once said you can wish in one hand and spit in the other and observe which hand gets filled up first.

Planning

He had tracked the big grizzly for seven straight hours
He was hungry with food getting low;
A thousand-pound griz with only one arrow
And shot from his sixty-pound bow.

Carefully scanning the woods for his foe
The bear quickly charged for a fight;
He was now very ready to drop that big teddy
And he raised up the bow with its sight.

But the hunter stopped dead, in his tracks, turned his head
His wits were now out of control;
For instead of the bow to launch his arrow
He was grasping his old fishing pole.

He knew right away the bear had his way
So he searched for an alternate route;
He would have been fine with his number 4 line
If the bear would have been a brook trout.

The lesson that day when he passed away
Is for every child, woman, and man;
To avoid needless strife and perhaps save your life
Always remember to plan.

Read this poem again and I truly hope, friend
That it serves as a tool to remind;
That one hour of planning can save you hours of scanning
For ways to protect your behind.

Perhaps you are thinking that story is ridiculous. No one would take a fishing pole instead of a bow and arrow. No one would be that stupid or careless. If you do have that thought in your mind, you are probably correct. No one would do anything as careless as that example. Well, I am not that sure. Working in public schools for thirty-eight years, I have seen students do things just as silly as the bear hunter.

I have had children sit in my office and tell me that they are wanting to graduate from high school. Upon questioning them about what they were doing to bring that to pass, I was somewhat surprised at some of their answers. "So you want to graduate from high school, do you?" "Yes, I do," they would affirm again. Then I would ask, "Do you attend school regularly?" "Well, no," they would respond. "Do you pay attention in

LES AND SHARON EDINGER

your classes? Do you behave well in school? Do you faithfully turn in your homework? Do you study? Do you ask serious questions in class? Do you prepare for your quizzes and tests?" To these questions many of these kids will respond, "No." Yes, they want to graduate from high school, but they do not do the very things that will make that possible. In a sense, they are like that bear hunter that went out with his fishing pole. Chances are they will not be any more successful than the hunter.

Stand in the middle of your living room and decide that you are going to walk out of the front door of your house. Count to three and then begin moving. But instead of taking steps toward your front door, step toward your back door. After taking about five or six steps, stop and survey the situation. Are you getting closer to your front door or to the back door? Obviously, the back door is the correct answer.

If you want to go to the front door, you must take the necessary steps that will get you to the front door. Likewise, if you want to reach your goals and dreams, you must take the necessary steps that take you closer to your goals and dreams. This is what plans and following those plans will do for you. One step at a time, one day at a time, and you will get closer and closer to fulfilling and achieving those goals. Without goals and plans, you are like that ship without a rudder. You are like the bear hunter with his fishing pole or the student that wants to graduate but refuses to attend school and study. With goals and plans, however, you can succeed; and you will eventually achieve the things that you planned.

A necessary step to take in achieving our goals and fulfilling our dreams is very basic and simple. It is simply to think about our goals and dreams every day. The Bible says, "As a man thinketh, so is he." Earl Nightingale says, "We become what we think about." Think. What can be more basic than that? People who are trainers of dolphins and seals spend a great deal of time thinking about dolphins, seals, and the training of sea animals. Doctors no doubt, before passing their medical exams, spend a great deal of time thinking about doctors, medicine, hospitals, and patients. Lawyers think about the law and courts, pilots think about flying, teachers think about schools and students, and generals think about the military. We do become what we think about.

So if you want to have something, if you want to become something, or if you want to do something special in the future, begin today to think about it and continue to think about it day after day until it becomes reality.

What do I mean when I say think about it? Suppose that your goal is to be trainer of animals at a place like Sea World. Then begin today by reading articles about the type of animals that are trained at Sea World. Visit Sea World when you get an opportunity and ask the people that work there for some advice on how to prepare. Take some courses in high school or college that will prepare you for that type of career. Subscribe to some magazines about sea life or the training of animals. Ask a local veterinarian about animals and get some tips from him or her. Visit your local library and read all the articles you can about things related to this type of work.

This is what I mean about thinking about your goals and dreams. If you truly have an interest in these areas, you will want to spend time doing these things, and it will come naturally to you. The more you think about these things related to your goals and the more you read about them, you will begin to find yourself getting closer and closer to achieving them. What you will be ten years from now, or what your life will be like then, all depends on what you entertain in your mind today. We become what we think about.

The Drunk and the Mayor

The mayor of your city and the drunk on the street
Both breathe the same air every day;
They hear the same songs and see the same sights
But their wallets show a difference of pay.

The trainer at Sea World and the nurse in your school
Had years of training I'll bet;
One works with dolphins while the other with kids
One remains dry, the other gets wet.

The girl at the counter in the restaurant downtown
And the robber downtown in the jail;
May both be smart people but the girl remains free
While the crook in his cell appears pale.

Why do people we know turn out as they do?
Why are humans so different and strange?
Why are there doctors, musicians, and cops?
Why do some herd the cows on the range?

Well, the mayor is the mayor for he thought of the city
And a bottle was the drunk's only wish;
The nurse thought of kids with their mumps and their lumps
And the trainer thought of dolphins and fish.

The girl at the counter thought of restaurants and cooking
While the robber thought of guns and of loot;
The doc thought of patients and musicians of music
And the wrangler thought of saddles and boots.

Do you get the picture of what I am saying?
Do you see your future this day?
If you think often enough of being a something
You'll turn out exactly that way.

Would you pilot a tank or coach a ball team
Or create a large food-eating chain;
Or perhaps you would rather forecast the weather
Well, you must put these thoughts in your brain.

If you can remember these facts, my dear friend,
Rising early each day from your bed;
You will see your life twenty years in the future
For the future begins in your head.

A life with goals can be compared to a garden that has been carefully planned from the beginning stages and weeded on a regular basis. It is neat, attractive, and pleasing to look upon. It is more productive than a garden that has been just thrown together with no plans of where the individual vegetables should be planted. Planting cucumbers too close to the tomatoes might cause some problems in weeding and harvesting the tomatoes because the cucumbers have a tendency to vine out and cover a rather large area.

Any gardener knows that if one doesn't weed the garden on a regular basis, other things, unwanted things will begin to grow on their own. If these unwanted plants are ignored for too long of a time, they not only reduce the harvest from the wanted plants but also actually choke out many of the good plants.

If we take control of our lives by establishing some solid goals to shoot for, make plans, and follow those plans to ensure that we reach those goals, then we will accomplish more worthwhile objectives in our lives in a few years than other people can in their entire lifetime. Without these goals and dreams in our lives, we will waste time, wander through life, and awake some morning and realize that we are sixty years old and wonder what do I have to show for my life.

The Garden

The young children stared at the odd-looking man
As he passed by the window at school;
The teacher couldn't keep the children's attention
As they hurried and climbed up on their stools.

For they just never saw a person before
With a dandelion growing out of one ear;
From his nose grew some crab grass and other strange weeds
They agreed that he looked mighty queer.

Up went their hands for permission to speak
They had questions for their teacher that day;
What caused such a thing in the life of that man?
And they listened to words she would say.

"Now, children, please listen and remember this day
The lesson that you're now going to learn;
For if you fail to succeed in learning these facts
Your life will be filled with concern.

"Did you ever observe your folks plant a garden
And work daily to keep out the weeds;
How they hoed, plucked, and pulled the unwanted plants
How they grew on their own with such speed?

"The crops that they wanted like corn and tomatoes
And beans, squash, peppers, and peas;
Had to fight for their space with the weeds growing tall
But the weeds always grew with such ease.

LES AND SHARON EDINGER

"The weeds didn't need planted and hoed
Nor watered or fertilized so;
They grew on their own and grew mighty fast
When the gardener just allowed them to grow.

"Well, the same thing happens to people you see
When they fail to tend to their brain;
When they don't plant the crops of thought and ambition
Or of plans for their goals to obtain.

"For when we just wander through life without goals
Without thoughts of a positive scope;
Then we're at the mercy of what grows in our minds
And we might just appear like a dope.

"Plant good and useful thoughts in your mind
To avoid countless troubles and strife;
Set some goals and make plans to follow your dreams
And you'll be a winner in life."

We only live once, and usually we only live on this planet for eighty to one hundred years. Make the best of it. If you have a specific career goal when you grow up, decide to become the best there is in that career. Do you want to be a dancer? Be an outstanding dancer. Do you want to be a newspaper journalist? Be the best one in the city. Be the best there is. Disraeli, a great philosopher, said, "Life is too short to be little."

Remember from the first section of this book, you can be the best because you have the potential of being or having or doing anything in this life that you decide you want. Why not take advantage of this. You owe it to yourself to have the best in life. God does not want us to live in poverty and be dependent on others. He wants us to take what we have and increase our belongings. He has made you responsible for the talents you possess. He expects you to take those talents and do everything you can to multiply that number. Go to the Bible and read that parable of the slothful servant who took his talent and buried it. His idea was that he would be less likely to lose his talent if he didn't use it. But it doesn't work that way.

We don't lose our talents by using them; we lose them by allowing them to lie dormant. So begin today and take those talents and gifts you have and put them to work by reaching for your goals and dreams.

What a tragedy it would be if some of the great ones in history had set lower goals for themselves. What if Paul Revere would have ridden just part of the way from Boston to the outlying towns on that historic night in 1775? What if Thomas Edison would have settled on a lightbulb that only stayed lit for three minutes? What if Michael Jordan decided that he was only good enough to play high school ball? What if the tiny nation of Israel decided that it was too small and weak to survive against the joint powers of the Arab world? What if the early creators of television had decided after a few failures that it was impossible to make that medium practical for individual families?

Thank heaven that the masters did set high goals and make plans to reach them. We have it so much easier than our founding fathers did. Winters are easier to survive in New England in 1997 than in the 1600s. It is easier to travel from New York to Los Angeles today than in 1860. Farmers can grow more today with fewer men and sweat than they could in 1776. Why? Over the years people like you and me set and achieved goals that made life easier for themselves and for everyone who would be born in the years to come.

Aim High

If Michelangelo's goals would have been a bit lower
Than the ones he had chosen in life;
Not a soul would remember his name nor his work
Not a child, not a husband, nor wife.

For if instead of the beautiful paintings up high
On the ceiling that folks just adore;
What if the great artist, as he entered that chapel
Just decided to paint on the floor.

We know that Columbus traveled over the ocean
To discover the land of the free;
For his goals said, "Go West," but with lesser ambition
He would have stayed in the Mediterranean Sea

And then there was Ford who built thousands of autos

His V8 made him famous, of course;
Now if he would have set smaller goals for himself
He might have traveled around on a horse.

And so, my dear friend, let us learn from these men
Your goals, set them high and don't stop;
To work hard every day and give it your best
Till you're standing tall at the top.

CHAPTER III

Persevere
(Don't Quit)

STEP 1 IS to believe in yourself, and the second step is to set those goals. The third and final step is to persevere until your goals are a reality. Then it will be time to set new goals and take off again. Don't quit. The English people didn't quit when Hitler was bombing them night and day during the Battle of Britain. Babe Ruth didn't quit after proving to the world that he was one of the greatest strikeout artists in the game of baseball. Lee Iacocca didn't quit after being fired by Ford. John Kennedy didn't quit after his PT boat was sunk from under him in the waters of the Pacific. And you must not quit either as you are pursuing your goals.

Some of your goals will be achieved easily with little effort and concern; but most of them will take some time, effort, and willpower on your part to continue. You are going to meet people that will try to discourage you. Along the way you are going to encounter failures, setbacks, and situations that would discourage many people. Welcome to life. Some call it the real world. But whatever you call it, remember, if you believe in yourself, set those goals and persevere. Life will eventually throw up her hands and say, "Buddy, you win."

History records thousands of examples of the power of perseverance. Perseverance or persistence will make up the difference if we fall short in the categories of skills, talent, or knowledge. Calvin Coolidge said,

> Nothing in the world can take the place of persistence.
> Talent will not. Nothing is more common than unsuccessful
> men with talent. Genius will not, unrewarded genius is almost a proverb.
> Education will not, the world is full of educated failures.
> Persistence and determination alone are omnipotent.

George Herman Ruth grew up in the streets of Baltimore. His father ran a saloon, and young George drifted in and out of trouble during his early years as a boy. The authorities finally placed George in a home for boys labeling him as incorrigible. He was loud, boisterous, and never hesitated to use his fists to help clarify his opinion on important topics. He would not have been an ideal choice if someone were looking for a man to write a book on manners and social graces. Sometimes he was crude, embarrassing, and extremely awkward in engagements in society.

The Babe, as he was known throughout his career, was also a loveable big guy with a heart as big as the world. He never forgot his difficult childhood, and kids always found a friend in him. He visited hospitals, entertained homeboys, and did many things to bring smiles to those kids that didn't have too much to smile about in their own world. The Babe was a true hero to countless thousands of kids across America.

While he was in that home for boys, he became a pitcher on the school's baseball team. Excelling there as a pitcher, George was discovered by major-league baseball. Later he ended up as a player for the New York Yankees. Because of his power as a batter, the Yankee manager transferred him to the outfield, and that permitted him to bat every day. The rest is history. Babe Ruth became one of the greatest baseball players in history, and his name will be spoken as long as people gather on diamonds and someone yells, "Play ball."

Not everyone is a Yankee fan. Many people came to the park to boo and harass the Bambino. They loved to see him swing and miss and to watch him throw his temper tantrums with the umpires. When Babe connected with a pitch, it was a picture of beauty to see his muscles ripple as pistons of power and send that ball into the bleachers. On the other hand, when he missed the ball, his body would sometimes turn clear around as if out of control due to some spasm; and he would tumble to the ground on both knees. When this would happen, his nonfans would rise to their feet and harmonize in a chorus of catcalls and laughter. Babe would rise to his feet, take his place back in the batter's box, and get ready for the next pitch.

Babe Ruth is known for hitting 714 home runs, a major-league record until it was broken by the also great Hank Aaron of the Atlanta Braves. On his way to becoming a home run king, Babe stuck out 1,330 times, also a major league record. His nonfans had plenty of opportunities to discourage the Babe, and they took full advantage of his failures at the plate. Many of these critics were some sports writers who showed little mercy for him as his number of strikeouts increased over the years.

But Babe Ruth is not known for his failures. He is not remembered for his strikeouts. He is known and remembered for his home runs and what home runs they were. They not only entered the bleachers, but many of them sailed over them and into the streets. His homers were so impressive that he was also referred to as the Sultan of Swat.

The Babe is a good example of what some people refer to as a successful failure. He failed so many times at the plate that he was a leader in strikeouts, but he didn't quit. He kept swinging day after day, week after week, and year after year until his name has been placed along with other baseball greats in Cooperstown, New York, the home of the Baseball Hall of Fame.

Keep Swinging

Babe Ruth stepped up to the plate each day
His body so massive and stout;
He swung with his might the bat in his hand
Three swings and the "Sultan" was out.

Day after day he returned to the plate
And continued to swing for the fence;
Continuing to miss the ball quite a bit
Many said that he had no sense.

But the Babe just smiled and swung away
And today when we mention his name;
It's his homers we think of, not his KOs
He's enshrined in the Hall of Fame.

So what if you fail and then fail again
All the great ones missed some connections;
There are stories of Edison's flops with his light
And Lincoln lost some elections.

So just like the Babe, take your time at the bat
And know, you can't always be winning;
You might lose now and then, buy you'll win in the end.
Just remember, always keep swinging.

LES AND SHARON EDINGER

We all have our share of failures. If we are trying to accomplish something worthwhile in life, we have one guarantee: we are going to have our share of failures. Instead of becoming discouraged and having these failures serve as a negative experience, count them as a blessing and learn from them. Just tell yourself, "Well, that didn't work out the way I hoped it would, so I'll just try it again." Remember, when we fail, we join the ranks of some of the world's great. Take some pride in knowing that your name is up there with Lincoln, Ruth, Edison, and Ford.

Failure. Is it such a bad word? Is failure always negative? Of course, not. We can't learn everything we need to know if we are winning all the time. Some things are only learned after we have fallen on our face a few times. Everything cannot be learned from a book. We learn some things only by trial and error.

Repeated failures and repeated attempts to try again not only teach us valuable lessons, but these attempts also toughen us up. Many people look back on their basic training in the army as a time "they would not trade for anything in the world," but they sure wouldn't want to go through it again. Why wouldn't they trade it? Because they realize that even though it was a difficult, miserable, and even painful experience, they are stronger and wiser today because of that basic training.

Every bad experience we have, painful as it may be at the present, can teach us valuable lessons and make us people of stronger character and backbone. That is why it may be great to have the education under one's belt, but when given an opportunity, many employers look for someone with some experience along with that education. Experience is a good teacher; and when we fail, fall on our face, come up with an empty hand, and hit rock bottom, we are much better off than someone who never tried at all. Yes, we are now stronger, wiser, more educated, and polished than we were when we started.

Struggles

The young girl stood for twenty-five minutes
And watched the cocoon in the tree;

She could see how it moved as the new butterfly
Tried its best to break out and be free.

She felt kind of sad of the monarch's great struggle
How tired and weak it must be;
For it worked very hard and its progress was slow
And she longed for its colors to see.

So she went to her house and brought back a knife
And carefully opened one end;
And out came the insect with its colors of gold
With its wings spreading out to the wind.

The butterfly flew a very short distance
To a branch just beyond the girl's head;
And there where it lit, it tottered a bit
Then fell to the ground, it was dead.

Trying to help this beautiful creature
By opening the cocoon with the knife;
The butterfly lost some exercise needed
And entered too early in life.

She should have allowed the insect to struggle
And break free of the cocoon without aid;
For that is the way they build up their strength
That's the way the strong ones are made.

And in life we will have our trials and problems
That will cause us some grief and concern;
Our struggles increase our strength and endurance
And in battles, there are lessons to learn.

So hold your head high, march forward with courage
To face all that life has in store;
And when opportunity knocks, being stronger and wiser
You'll be able to open its door.

LES AND SHARON EDINGER

Thomas Edison failed over ten thousand times when he was working on the electric light. Many of the leading scientists of his day thought that there was no future in electricity as a source of light in the home, but Edison continued to experiment. Someone asked him why he continued after failing so many times. Edison replied, "You don't understand. I have not failed at all. I have successfully identified ten thousand ways that will not work. That has put me ten thousand times closer to the one that will work." So he continued, and the rest is history.

Wilma Rudolph, a lady track star of the sixties, suffered an illness as a child that left her legs damaged and almost useless as limbs. Many people wondered if she would ever be able to walk again, even with braces. Even the doctors thought that Wilma would never be able to walk with any degree of normalcy. She would probably live her life out in a small town in Tennessee. She would be known only to her family, neighbors, and friends that she would encounter in that area.

But no one had measured the heart of this young black girl. With her braces and with months of exercise and torture, she finally was able to walk short distances. She continued to walk and exercise until she was able to do it without the braces. On and on she walked and even experimented with running short distances. Pleased with the joy she received from running, she continued to run.

This teenage girl, who many thought would spend most of her time on the front porch, ended up on the front page of newspapers throughout the world. Why? Her running earned a scholarship at the University of Tennessee. In 1960 she represented the United States in the Olympic Games in Rome, Italy.

Some critics took one look at this skinny black girl representing the United States and wondered why we would send her to represent our nation. As they watched young Wilma warm up, they noticed that she walked with a slight limp. What right did she have participating with the great athletes of the world? This was the contest of all contests, and only the world's finest dare compete. Why would we send someone like this to line up on the starting line with the champions of other nations? What right did she have competing in the one hundred meters? Well, it only took a few seconds after the gun cracked for these critics to get their answer. She was the one standing on the center platform as the Star-Spangled Banner was raised to our national anthem. She was the one who lowered her head and allowed the Olympic officials to place a gold medal around her neck. Wilma Rudolph was a champion who refused to quit when things became difficult. If she proved to be a winner in life, then so can you. Never, ever, give up.

No, No

No, David, no, Goliath is too big
Why you're just a boy not a man;
None of our warriors will challenge his might
Now leave and go home while you can.

But David determined to win on that day
With faith and a plan in his head;
Marched forward as the giant missed with his spear
Then with a rock, he struck the foe dead.

No, Roger, no, a four-minute mile
No man could survive at that pace;
Year after year the experts agreed
No man could run such a race.

But when the gun cracked, young Roger took off
For years he had trained for this trial;
And today upon reading of Bannister's life
He has busted that four-minute mile.

No, Thomas, no, electric won't do
To make a light that is useful for man;
You have already failed over ten thousand times
You're a fool if you think that you can.

But he continued to work on his dream
Till his lab lit up through the night;
And today the world is a much-brighter place
For Tom has invented the light.

LES AND SHARON EDINGER

No, Wilma, no, I'm afraid you won't walk
Without braces giving strength to your feet;
The muscles are weakened in both of your legs
Why to try and compete means defeat.

Wilma Rudolph ignored all the voices of doom
Walking on and even running I'm told;
And later in Rome as she stood tall and proud
Around her neck was placed a ribbon with gold.

Well, what about you? Have you ever been told
That your plans are just a foolish man's scheme?
You're too slow or too old or too young to succeed
Just quit and give up on your dream.

Well, remember, my friend, you don't need their approval
You're the one that determines the score;
Decide what you want out of life and keep trying
And I promise, you'll receive even more.

If you want to want to accomplish something, find other people that have already accomplished that something and learn from them. We do not have to reinvent the wheel. Many of the things that we would like to do have already been achieved by others. Read the lives of successful people. There are not many books written about the losers in life. My definition of a loser is very simple. A loser is a person that has failed at something and then quit. Everyone fails, but the losers quit trying. This is the end of their story. The winners fail, try again, fail, try again, and keep trying until they have succeeded. So if you want to be a winner, read about the successful failures in life.

Maybe you don't have to read about them. Perhaps all you need to do is ask your parents or your neighbors or your teachers or your friends what they have done that enabled them to succeed with their dreams. If you want to earn a certain amount of money, seek advice from people that have already earned that same amount of money. If you want to build a beautiful home, seek advice from people who already have the house of their dreams. If you want to be a winner, seek advice from the winners of life. Don't go to the losers.

Most people don't follow this advice. They have a dream in their heart and start out on the road to reach that dream, and then someone comes along and bursts their bubble. They might say that "you are too old" or "too young" or that "no one else has ever done that." Well, don't listen to people like that. If your dream is to own a beautiful Jaguar, chances are that the people who might tell you that you will never achieve that dream don't have a Jaguar themselves. A person that owns one won't laugh at you or try to put you down because he/she knows that it is possible because he/she already has one.

Be Careful Where You Go

Don't go to the grocer if you're shopping for autos
You just won't have any luck;
Don't hunt in Death Valley with its arid white sand
And hope for your limit of ducks.

Don't sail in the ocean with its waters so blue
If searching for your wandering cat;
Don't visit the bakery and eat all you see
If you're trying to lose all your fat.

Don't go to the mountains if you're looking for dolphins
I never saw any that high;
Don't go to the teller at 7-Eleven
If you broke the bone in your thigh.

And don't go to the man who never is happy
For advice on the pleasures of life;
And don't go to your neighbor for advice on your marriage
If he is running around on his wife.

And don't go to the person that's afraid to take risks
For advice on fulfilling your dream;

LES AND SHARON EDINGER

And don't ask the jock for some tips on persistence
When disgruntled, he walked off the team.

But when needing some help or advice with a problem
Go to someone who's succeeded before;
Do this with a grin and I guarantee friend
The treasures of life are in store.

Yes, go to the winners in life for advice and for inspiration. And as I previously mentioned, most of these winners are also the successful failures. Abraham Lincoln lost several elections, failed in business, lost in love, and never knew a day of peace during his years in the White House. Abraham Lincoln is also considered by many people to have been the greatest president in our nation's history.

Helen Keller, blind and deaf her entire life, had an extremely difficult childhood and was considered by many people as uncooperative and unteachable. And yet this lady overcame unbelievable odds and became one of the most competent, educated, and respectable figures of the twentieth century.

Mel Tillis, a man that stutters with every sentence that he speaks and has done so since he was a child, is one of the most popular country Western artists today. He is popular for two reasons. First, he does a remarkable job singing as the words flow from his lips without a flaw. He has learned to sing beautifully without the interference of stuttering and has recorded several albums and has made hundreds of personal appearances throughout the nation.

The second reason that he has won the hearts of millions is that when he is interviewed in person or on television, he doesn't try to hide the fact that he has a problem with stuttering. He is open about his problem, and people can clearly see the difficulty that he has when speaking. This has inspired many people and encouraged others with similar afflictions.

Lincoln, Keller, and Tillis are just three examples of people who had more than their share of problems; and yet they refused to throw in the towel. These are true examples of successful failures. Whatever difficulties you encounter, make up your mind that you are going to follow the examples of these three remarkable people.

Dues

Have you ever been fired or passed over at work
For a raise that should have been yours?
Have you ever been broke or have lost all your money
When you wanted to have shopped in some stores?
Have you ever been sad and felt very bad?
Have you ever been mad, my lass or my lad
When opportunity has locked all its doors?

Have you ever been scared as you made a decision?
Have you ever been frightened at night?
Have you ever been lost or broken down on the road
Or have been forced to stand up and fight?
Have you ever been blue or down sick with the flu?
Have some treated you like a worn-out old shoe
While they live a life of delight?

Have you even been laughed at or put down by your friends?
Have you ever been cheated or beat?
Have you ever been puzzled when left with a problem?
Have you ever been knocked off your feet?
Have you ever been stumped or by a bully been thumped?
Have you ever been bumped and left with a lump?
Have you ever been kicked in your seat?

Then stand up and cheer for luck's on your side
For others have traveled this road;
For some special people have had the same breaks
In the books, their stories are told.
Just read about Lincoln, Helen Keller, and Ford
Wilma Rudolph for years couldn't walk;
But she won gold medals by running in Rome
And Mell Tillis, well, he just couldn't talk.
Beethoven was deaf when he wrote his great classics
Ray Charles sings on without sight
So when you have some problems and the world puts you down

LES AND SHARON EDINGER

Go forward and continue to fight.
And just like these winners whose names you've just read
You'll stand taller and wiser each day;
These trials will build your strength and endurance
These are the dues you must pay.

It isn't much fun when you are hoping for a home run and instead you strike out. It takes courage to continue when you are singing on stage, and you forget your lines. Many people have given up the idea of getting a ham radio license after failing a Morse code test. It never is easy to continue to try after repeated attempts followed by repeated failures. How do some people find the ability to keep on trying after so many rejections, failures, or nos?

Colonel Sanders was in his sixties and had little money to invest when he started his Kentucky Fried Chicken enterprise. The only two assets he had going for him was a recipe for chicken and a dream of becoming wealthy. He took his recipe from restaurant to restaurant and asked the owners to take a chance on his chicken. He was told, "*No,*" time and time again. How many nos would you listen to before you decided to give up? Ten? Fifty? One hundred? Five hundred? The Colonel was told *no* 1,009 times before he got his first *yes.* Talk about a successful failure. There are few better examples than Colonel Sanders.

What kept him going after experiencing so many rejections? It was because he did not focus on the *nos* he was getting. He kept focusing on his goal and dream to be a success someday and what it would be like to own a successful chain of restaurants. Today there is a Kentucky Fried Chicken restaurant in every city of any size throughout the United States.

Why did Edison continue to experiment with the electric light after failing over ten thousand times? He did not worry about all those failures. He kept thinking of the time when electric lights would brighten the streets of this country from coast to coast. In other words, like Sanders, he concentrated on his goals, not the obstacles. We must learn to do the same.

Do you wish to learn how to play the guitar? If you do, you cannot be overwhelmed with the sore fingers you are going to experience from pressing down on the strings. You need to think of the music that you are going to play and the friends you will be entertaining. Focus on the product, not on the problems you are bound to encounter along the way. The problems will come and go, and if you stick with your plans and refuse to quit, you will accomplish more in your life than the average Joe citizen.

Keep Your Eyes on Your Dreams

"I hope I don't hit that wall to my right,"
The driver said time and again.
"And I hope I don't hit that car to my left
That just wouldn't do for a win."

And as he proceeded to avoid a collision
His heart beating faster each sec;
His eyes kept shifting from the wall to the car
Till *bang!!* He had a terrible wreck.

Instead of fixing his eyes on that wall
Or on the car that troubled him so;
He should have been looking at the space in the middle
For that's where he wanted to go.

Bill stepped to the foul line and was handed the ball
And he glanced at the net and the rim;
But his mind was upon the noise of the crowd
And the cheers of the folks in the gym.

He didn't focus on the goal with its net
And missing, he went down in defeat;
With his head bent low he returned to his bench
And Bill slithered down in his seat.

And Peter was thrilled to see the dear Master
Walking out on the waves in the sea;
So Peter stepped out of the boat and proceeded
To walk to the Lord with much glee.

LES AND SHARON EDINGER

At first he successfully walked out on the water
With his mind firmly focused you see;
On the man that was known as the carpenter's son
What a sight there in old Galilee.

But soon Peter's mind wandered a bit
From the King to the waves tossing high;
And his thoughts centered now on the depths of the ocean
In despair then he started to cry.

What can we learn from these three short examples?
The message is simple and clear;
Focus upon your goals and ambitions
Not the problems you encounter each year.

You will find your shares of trials and problems
As you go through the years of your life;
With sickness, pain, despair, and some failures
You'll encounter many faces of strife.

But don't dwell on them but rather your goals
Go forward with a heart full of steam;
Till you overcome all the trials facing you
And enjoy your heart's biggest dream.

Some people fail to reach their goals because of the obstacles they have to overcome to reach them. Sometimes it isn't easy, but those who persevere and accomplish their goals realize that the final rewards far surpass all the obstacles put together. That is why it is so important for you to focus your attention on your dreams. But overcoming the obstacles isn't the only reason some people never fulfill their biggest dreams. Some people are so tied to the past that they find it extremely difficult to grab on to the future. Change is a scary thing to many people.

We are so accustomed to the present that we worry about the changes that tomorrow will bring. Will I get along with the new people that I am going to meet? Will I be able to handle the extra responsibility? What will people think if I try and then fail? What if I have to relocate? Will I be happy in the new area? Will I be happy with the change in my life?

Change? If we have one guarantee in life, it is this. Tomorrow will bring change. Life is constantly changing. The only people that don't experience change are the people that are living in the cemeteries. Change is going to occur anyway. Why not do what you can to control that change. That is why having goals and making plans are so important. With goals and plans, we take charge of the future and control most of the changes that are going to happen to us. Without these goals and plans, we are at the mercy of others. We are at the mercy of current events, and we will have little or no control of our lives in the future. Remember, only people with goals and plans are truly free. The others are slaves to the goals and dreams of others.

Don't be afraid of the future and the unknown. As you set your goals and begin to follow your plans, your life is going to change. It is going to change by taking you closer and closer to the place where your heart and mind are pointing to. Don't be afraid. Be happy and excited about this new adventure. Be excited because you are going to go where most people only dream about. You are going to the towns called Successville and Achievement City.

Letting Go

The circus was here and the big top was crowded
Thousands were present to see;
The bears on their bikes, the clowns and their fights
Oh, the children, how they shouted with glee.

There were horses and dogs and fancy dressed hogs
There were monkeys and elephants too;
Lions and cats, bearded ladies so fat

LES AND SHARON EDINGER

It really was quite the to-do.

The crowd was real pleased when the elephant sneezed
And the clowns all fell down in a row;
The ponies were prancing while the dogs started dancing
This was a very, very talented show.

But the greatest of joy of each girl and boy
Was when they saw people flying in air;
Way up toward the roof with artists aloof
The trapeze was the hit of the fair.

How graceful up there as she moved through the air
Holding on to her chum on his bar;
Then letting go of his hands with a somersault grand
And catching a swing from afar.

Time and again the girl and her friend
Swung high o'er the noise of the tent;
And cheers were so loud that the folks in the crowd
Became silent when their voices were spent.

And now comes our turn for a lesson to learn
From the folks on the flying trapeze;
They were the hit of the show for they learned to let go
And reach out for the swing with such ease.

They could not complete this inspiring feat
If they failed to let go of their friend;
And reach out with belief that success and relief
Would be waiting for them in the end.

Remember, my friend, that success in the end
Comes to those who have courage at last;
To grab on to tomorrow, with laughter or sorrow
And are able to let go of the past.

Sometimes with clenched fists we need to take risks
And move upward to prove that we are;
Worthy and willing our dreams of fulfilling
Of hitching our swing to a star.

During World War II, John F. Kennedy's PT Boat was cut in half by a Japanese ship. Two men were dead and some were injured. John Kennedy helped one crew member that was badly burned swim to shore. For several days the crew of the PT Boat suffered from hunger, pain, and the fear that can overwhelm one in that type of a situation. Each night they would take turns swimming back out to sea, hoping to signal a U.S. ship that might pass by. Since Kennedy was the skipper, he had to help his crew overcome the physical obstacles that they were facing. He also had the even more difficult task to help them with their mental and emotional problems during these days of pure hell that they were experiencing. With his leadership and guidance, the crew did survive until help came; and less than twenty years later, John F. Kennedy was sworn in as the president of the United States. If John Kennedy would have given up during those difficult days on that island in the South Pacific, he never would have been elected as president, and that could have greatly altered our history. It was John Kennedy that stood toe-to-toe with Nikita Khrushchev during the Cuban Missile Crisis in the early sixties.

During the Civil War, the South was usually outnumbered in battle. The Union army also had the advantage of having more weapons and better transportation to move its soldiers from one battlefield to the next. The South was also at the disadvantage of having fewer factories and industries that manufactured war materials. The North had so many advantages that many people thought the war would last only a few weeks and the southern states would stop their rebellion and reenter the union.

But these critics who thought the Confederates would be an easy pushover just didn't calculate the hearts of the men that wore the grey uniforms. Lee, Jackson, Hood, and Stewart were four examples of soldiers that knew that a rifle and a pouch of ammunition were not the most important weapons to carry into a battle. They knew that as long as their men believed they could win, they would be a force to reckon with on the field of battle.

That is why at the Battle of Bull Run, Jackson stepped into the history books forever as one of his fellow officers shouted at his soldiers, "Look, men, there is Jackson holding his line like a stone wall." Ever since that day at Bull Run when the outnumbered Confederate forces defeated the Northern troops, Jackson has been known as Stonewall Jackson. He refused to quit; he refused to enter battle with a negative attitude. Later when General Robert E. Lee was told that Jackson had been wounded and had to have his arm amputated, Lee said, "Jackson has lost his left arm, and I have lost my right." The war didn't end in a few days, weeks, or months. It took four long years and hundreds of thousands of casualties before Lee surrendered to Grant.

With a poor attitude and the habit of quitting when things get difficult, a person is going to remain an average Joe citizen and never experience the joys and thrills of accomplishing something truly remarkable. On the other hand, with a positive attitude and the "I'll never quit" habit, a person is going to accomplish more in five or ten years than most people accomplish in a lifetime. Which type of person are you going to be? I will repeat, you only live once. Why not go for it all! Give life your best shot! Think big! Be positive with the I-can-do-it frame of mind; and you will be one of the leaders in your neighborhood, city, state, or nation.

The Pool

Young Beth and her father went swimming each day
At the local community pool;
The girl tried to learn how to swim like her dad
But she couldn't and she felt like a fool.

Day after day she practiced her strokes
With friends who lived on the same block;
Yes, she worked very hard but when left all alone
She sank to the depths like a rock.

Her friends laughed and mocked her day after day
While her father looked on with concern;
Poor Beth was beginning to lose faith in herself
And she wondered if she ever would learn.

Beth's father continued to encourage his girl
As he oiled her back for a tan;
"You can do it, my daughter, just keep on trying."
And Beth finally said, "Yes, I can!"

Then one day her friends walked up to the pool
And saw a most interesting sight;
A girl like a fish out in the deep water
Was laughing with shouts of delight.

Young Beth still resembled the gal they all knew
Her eyes, freckles, dimples, and all;
This was the girl that sank like a sinker
But today she was having a ball.

Beth hadn't grown any fins or a tail
She still was that beautiful lass;
She didn't have scales, no fishylike smells
Beth looked like a girl, not a bass.

What allowed her to swim wasn't found on her body
Her dad being patient and kind;
Knew that key to learning to swim
Was the birth of a positive mind.

There are two more areas I need to cover in this book that will have a great impact upon your life. If you make the right decision in these two areas, they will greatly increase your chances of a successful life. First, to fully maximize your talents and ambitions, you need to master the art of getting along with people. I would recommend that you read Dale Carnegie's book *How to Win Friends and Influence People*. This is a masterpiece, and I believe that every high school student in this country should be required to pass a test on the contents of this book prior to receiving a diploma. He titled the first chapter "If You Want to Gather Honey, Don't Kick over the Hive!!" To help me remember the important aspects of this chapter, I created this little jingle.

LES AND SHARON EDINGER

Don't kick the hive over if you're after the honey
Why it just makes the honeybees mad.
Getting stung is no fun and eating the hon with a pain in your bun
Oh really, it's nothing but sad.

And when working with people be friendly and kind
And you'll find as the years pass by;
That you are farther ahead and happier too
By being the likeable guy.

Trying to be a success in life without people skills is like being a surgeon and fainting at the sight of blood. Learning how to be a good listener and a good conversationalist will open more doors for you than all of the keys in the world. Being polite is not just considered good manners; it is good business. During the industrial age, hard work alone could put food on the table and clothes on one's back. But today in the information age, we need to fine-tune our people skills if we have hope of greatly improving our station in life.

Surgeons need to possess great skills when operating on a patient. Truck drivers also have skills to master if they are going to make a career of driving those 18 wheelers across this nation. Pilots need to skillfully fly those planes away from one airport and then land them again safely at a distant airport. Just being able to find those distant airports thousands of miles away takes skill and training. Every job on earth requires some type of skill. The most important skill on earth, however, is the art of knowing how to get along with other people. Surgeons, truck drivers and pilots encounter people every day on their job and being able to favorably interact with these people is a must.

Getting Along

The most important skill on this planet
Should be taught in the homes and the schools;
For people who never master this art
Are considered and labeled the fools.

Getting along with folks from all walks of life
Is a skill the wisest have taught;
For men and women possessing this gift
Are the ones the masters have sought.

Just take a few notes and practice a bit
And soon your neighbors will see;
A genuine friend, a leader of men
A buddy, a winner you'll be.

PEOPLE DON'T CARE HOW MUCH YOU KNOW
TILL THEY KNOW HOW MUCH YOU CARE
If you can transmit your caring sincere
Your table will never be bare.

Would you like to get the other's attention
Are you seeking some fortune or fame;
Then do this with people you meet every day
REMEMBER, REMEMBER THEIR NAME.

And another tip to remember, my friend
When conversing with folks that you meet;
With two open ears and only one mouth
LISTEN MUCH MORE THAN YOU SPEAK

What if your opinions are different from theirs?
WELL, DON'T ARGUE WHATEVER YOU DO;
You can put on the act and prove every fact
And still end up in a stew.

There is another point to remember, my friend.
BE FRIENDLY AND PATIENT AND NICE
To all that you meet on porch, route, and street
You'll never get better advice.

One more area that is a must is stay away from drugs and alcohol. Far too many people have ruined their lives or have failed to reach their potential because of booze or pills. Alcohol has caused more heartaches, put more people in the hospital or the funeral home, destroyed more property, and brought more tears than any other evil in our society. It has killed more people in peace time than all the wars combined since time began.

LES AND SHARON EDINGER

Many people with superior talents and charisma have fallen victim to these two villains. Elvis Presley, the King, died years before he should have because of his addiction to pills. Hank Williams, the country music star of the '40s and '50s died at the age of twenty-nine because of his problem with alcohol and drugs. John Belushi, the sensational comedian that won the admiration of millions, was cut down in his prime by an overdose.

I know of two men in my community who were both track stars in high school. They both should have gone on to college on athletic scholarships. Perhaps they could have been good enough to compete in the Olympic Games. One is in his grave because his liver was destroyed by years of abusing his body with alcohol. The other still lives. Even though we have been acquainted for nearly forty years, he sometimes has a problem remembering my name and even his own. You see, his brain was partially destroyed by drug abuse.

Examples like these can be found in every community in every state in this nation. Booze and drugs. Shun them. Despise them and help others to wake up and smell the roses. No one can tinker with these demons for any length of time and come away unscathed.

The Truth about Booze and Drugs

Have you ever turned on the TV
And seen a sports star drinking some beer;
And heard him say that "this stuff tastes great
I've been chugging it down for years"?

Did you know that he gets paid to say that?
And he's just telling you part of the tale.
For many I fear drink too much of the beer

And have to spend time in jail.

They may be standing with a beautiful woman
With a smile and glass in their hands.
"This is the reason that I've had a good season
This is the best of the brands."

But they don't show you the thousands of others
Throwing up in their damaged, wrecked cars;
Or the scars that exist on their heads and their fists
From fighting with drunks in the bars.

They don't show you the children they are missing
From broken homes because of the brew;
They don't show you the pain and the misery
And depression to them isn't new.

They don't tell you of the thousands of victims
Slain by drivers that are drinking that beer;
They don't show the heartbroken parents
At Christmas at the end of the year.

And no one has won the great Heisman
While plastered and dizzy for hours
Why if the coach would appear while he's drinking a beer
The star would be sent to the showers.

So don't believe the lies that they tell you
Booze and drugs can cause you much strife;
Be a real *pro*, learn to say *no*!
Live a long and happier life.

I hope that you enjoyed reading this book, and more importantly, I hope that you found something within these few pages that can be of some help to you. If something did ring a bell in your head and made an impression, pass it along to someone else. I believe that we are on this earth for several reasons, and the number one purpose of us being here is to help each other. Helping each other. Zig Ziglar, an outstanding motivational

LES AND SHARON EDINGER

speaker says, "You can get anything in life you want, if you will just help enough other people get what they want." What a profound statement. Why not put it to practice in your life? Get some of Zig Zigler's tapes or books. He has helped countless thousands, and he can be an enormous source of inspiration for you.

Helping Each Other

It isn't much fun when you're sick with a fever
Or when headaches are pounding all day;
Or when you're driving a nail
And instead of success,
Your thumb just gets in the way.

Have you ever broken an arm or a leg
Or have carelessly yielded a knife?
And instead of slicing the turkey or ham
You came close to shortening your life.

Why do we have accidents, sickness, and pain
Why does God allow suffering to be?
The answer is worthy of deep contemplation
His reasons are sacred you see.

When we see our neighbor down with the flu
Or with troubles that life has in store;
We can relate to the trials she's bearing
For we've also had trials before.

So hopefully these problems will bring us together
As together we go through life;
And together we'll help each other along
As together we battle the strife.

Hand in hand as we travel this journey
Our Father will say from above;
I am pleased that they're helping each other
They have learned the meaning of love.

Remember, believe in yourself. Set some goals and make specific plans to reach those goals. The third thing to do, then, is make up your mind that no matter what happens, you are not going to throw in the towel. You are not going to quit and cry uncle. No, you are going to follow the examples of the successful failures in life, and you are going to continue to pursue those goals until you have reached them.

Believe in yourself    Set a goal or target   Persevere

B●P

TO THE

TOP